ANA'S GIRLS

The Essential Guide to the Underground Eating Disorder Community Online

by

Eda R. Uca

authorHOUSE

1663 Liberty Drive, Suite 200
Bloomington, Indiana 47403
(800) 839-8640
www.authorhouse.com

This book is a work of non-fiction. Names of people and places have been changed to protect their privacy.

First published by AuthorHouse 08/03/04

ISBN: 1-4184-9318-X (e)
ISBN: 1-4184-3795-6 (sc)

Library of Congress Control Number: 2004094176

Printed in the United States of America
Bloomington, Indiana

This book is printed on acid-free paper.

Disclaimer

This book does not promote eating disorders. The purpose of displaying the following information is not to justify self-destructive behavior but rather to expose the undeniable fact that thousands of young people are struggling in isolation with very real, life threatening disorders and we, as a society have not been able to properly help them. By shutting down their sites or throwing away this book, we do not eliminate the problem. Instead, we choose to ignore their cry and lose the opportunity to gain potent insight into their world. Unless we are willing to understand those with eating disorders, we are not going to eradicate this plague on our community.

The content of this book is often ugly, frightening and dangerous. However ignoring the content, or perhaps worse, employing a moralistic, emotive knee-jerk reaction to it, does not make it untrue to those who created the content. The author does not claim to agree with the attitudes or motivations of the underground eating disorder community on the internet. She does not validate their behavior nor does she claim to believe in the rationalized philosophies which some members of the online community use to validate their behavior. The author's interest is in displaying their behavior and philosophies in order to foster an environment of empathy, respect and fruitful open discussion on the issues. The author strongly believes that no social issue can properly be addressed unless all parties have their voices heard. We have not until this point had a venue in which the undiluted voice of this community was able to reach the general public. This book is that venue.

The author beseeches the reader not to vilify those who created the content of this book. They are our children, our spouses, our sisters and brothers, our patients and our students; they are represented in every class and race. No community is sheltered from this pain. That they suffer in silence does not relinquish our responsibility to them. No community is complete without their health. Let us take the first step towards becoming whole by hearing their cry.

Acknowledgements

This book would not have been possible without the support of countless beautiful people. A few of them are mentioned here.

Jaci, Marna, Ali, and many others who courageously invited me into their world: My greatest hope is that I have proven my worth of their trust and done justice to their cause.

My family: who provided me with every opportunity, except for the opportunity to fail. I could not have finished this project without their love and faith. If I have made them proud, then I have succeeded.

Lydia Esslinger: my surrogate school-day mom, for encouraging me to learn how to read, write and speak effectively.

Dr. Lisa Meyer: who formally introduced me to the world of sociological inquiry and subsequently changed the course of my life.

Angela Nicolella: For coming through in the final hour. Few could hope to match her generosity and talent.

Jaye Arrigenna: for her awesome kindness, patience, generosity, wisdom and support.

Elizabeth Boylan: my sociological soul-mate and dear friend.

Meaghan Masini, my best friend and partner-in-crime, and The Masini Family: who loved and supported me even when I did not make it easy to do so. They deserve to share in my success.

And, Rocky Anthony Mazzaferro: who believed.

This book is dedicated to anyone who feels misunderstood and anyone who strives to understand.

Table of Contents

Words and Symbols

As with any sub-group of society or counter-culture, the online eating disorder community has a unique vernacular. The following words are therefore defined according to the meaning held within the community and may contradict previously defined medical terminology.

Ana: Short for anorexia. Can describe a type of lifestyle, a disease, a person or is referred to as the embodiment of anorexic life; i.e. to call on Ana or Goddess Ana. It is sometimes distinguished from anorexia as a more benign descriptor of behavior.

Binge: To eat a subjectively large amount of food. It is often unplanned and is accompanied by low self-control. Shame, guilt and self-loathing are often felt by the binger after the incident. It often precedes purging, and especially precedes purging if the binge was planned. (See purge)

B&P: Stands for binge and purge. (See binge; purge)

BMI: Acronym for Body Mass Indicator. It is used as a measure of success and a better online description of size than weight alone because it includes height in its calculation. 17.5 is considered anorexic which 15 is considered emaciated. Most aim for a BMI between those values.

(704.7 x weight in lbs)/ (height in inches^2)

C.O.E.: Acronym for Compulsive Overeater. While it is an eating disorder in its own right, many anas and mias describe periods of overeating or binging as "going c.o.e." It entails feeling unable to control food cravings, or stick to an eating schedule. Often those going c.o.e. eat irrespective of hunger or desire for specific food being ingested and consume food past their physical comfort level. It is accompanied by feelings of incredible shame, guilt and self-loathing. It is often done in private.

Good Ring: A ring worn to remind one of their goals in respect to body modification. It must be removed before a binge because binging is not considered good behavior.

Mia: Short for bulimia. Can describe a lifestyle, a disease, a person or the embodiment of the above when capitalized. Has a less positive connotation than Ana. Is often suffered through rather than celebrated like Ana. Similar to ana, mia may be used to describe a more benign state that bulimia.

Negative Calorie Foods: Those foods which in the process of digestion force the body to use more calories than are in the food. There is disagreement over whether they truly exist and what they might be. As a general rule of thumb, they are crunchy fruits and vegetables. These are considered "safe foods" regardless. (See safe foods)

Purge: To voluntarily vomit, often after binging (especially if the person identifies themselves as Ana) but sometimes after the ingestion of any food (especially if the person identifies themselves as Mia).

Red Bracelet: A red band symbolizing Ana and ana solidarity and sisterhood. Used by anas to identify each other. May be bought on websites or made at home.

Safe Food: Food which may be eaten with relatively low guilt due to high nutrient content or low fat or calorie content. Examples are fruits or vegetables. (Also see negative calorie foods.)

Thinspiration: Generally anything that inspires one to strive for thinness. Can take many forms, including but not limited to, pictures, quotes and stories. May be positive or embody ideals of thinness (i.e. a picture of a supermodel) or may be negative (i.e. a story of death due to binging).

Trigger: An external stimulus which can lead to a change in behavior. Often something that encourages anorexic or bulimic behavior, for example, a thinspirational picture. May be positive or negative in value and effect. (See thinspiration)

Unsafe Food: Those foods which are especially difficult for the body to process and are a hindrance to weight loss. Examples are cream (which is high in fat content and considered to be intestine-clogging) and chocolate (which is not only high in fat but also in relative calorie content and is thought to trigger binges). (See trigger, binge)

2468: A diet method used to avoid stagnation of weight loss. Aims to speed the metabolism by varying caloric intake. Variation is found in method but generally the dieter ingests 200 calories on the first day and then consequently ingests 400, 600 and 800. The cycle may be completed with a day of zero calorie ingestion (fasting). It is stressed that extra calories on later days are to come from increased ingestion of fruits or vegetables.

Basic Elements of All Groups

Almost all sites, irrespective of philosophy, are based on the same format and include the same headings for information. These headings universally indicate what type of information is on each link. Warning and Recovery groups have a similar format but will be dealt with in another section.

Disclaimer: All sites use disclaimers to warn that their sites contain triggering images and information (see trigger) and that they believe in personal responsibility and having given fair warning to readers, relinquish responsibility for the reader's behavior. Also this space is used, similar to those websites which display pornographic material, to give a reader who may not agree with the content a chance to avoid it.

Furthermore it is asked that any unsupportive readers refrain from harassing the webmaster/ mistress or supporters of the site.

Sacred Texts: Remarkably, this community has developed several texts which embody the mission, devotion, motivation and rules that members live by. These sacred texts appear so widely on websites that they are markers of membership to the community; all legitimate websites include one, if not all of these texts. These texts include "A letter from Ana", "Ana Creed" and "Ana Psalm." These texts are listed without an author, making them part of the community's mythology as well.

Tips & Tricks: Included under this heading is any combination of how to keep oneself from eating, how to avoid food oriented events (from nightly family dinners to birthday parties), how to cope with hunger, fatigue, dizziness and other symptoms of starvation, how to hide anorectic or bulimic behavior, excuses to avoid recovery, the quickest methods of weight loss and most effective exercise methods, what to do before, during and after a binge to allow for easy purging and how to purge. Also included may be product listings and ratings (i.e. the best diet pills or supplements).

Nutrition Information: Groups use this area to share survival tactics. This information is often accompanied by humor and reassurance to break through the reader's food anxieties. Titles such as "A Good Anorexic Never Dies!" grant those persisting in disordered behavior the permission to care for their basic needs. Included in this section are lists of calorie dense foods, the purpose of vitamins and minerals, the importance of proper hydration and lists of safe foods. Sites also use this section also to display calories and fat content of foods and list unsafe foods.

Thinspiration: All sites actively display a variety of thinspirational tools. These tools can take a wide range of forms including but not limited to pictures and photographs, quotes and lyrics, reading lists and movie lists, personal success stories, poetry and prose.

The thinspiration is graded on two scales. The first is in positive or negative values. According to this first scale thinspiration may inspire fear by displaying vilified symbols of failure, such as pictures of obese women or medical reports of death induced by binging. In contrast to these negatively valued tools, thinspiration may inspire hope by displaying glorified symbols of success such as pictures of emaciated fashion icons.

The second scale for thinspiration is more subtle and relies on the level of dedication or disorder of the intended audience. Accordingly, thinspiration may be more or less graphic. Groups that aim for emaciation will be more likely to display photographs of women suffering malnutrition whereas groups that aim for a more mainstream ideal of beauty will post photographs of celebrities such as Britney Spears. Britney Spears and other pop culture icons are an excellent defining point of dedication or disorder. There are camps which swear by these icons as role models and other camps which find these icons to be "too healthy" or even "too fat". In fact those groups which reject the mainstream ideal of beauty also mock those which embrace it for being imposters in the community.

Level of graphic thinspiration does not follow a clear trend within the factions. For example, some pro-ana groups may embrace the mainstream ideal as a healthy medium of attainable beauty while other pro-ana groups feel that the mainstream ideal is settling for mediocrity. The latter pro-anas state that "the human form, like sculpting, is brought to perfection when nothing is left to take away." So these more dedicated or disordered pro-anas are likely to display higher levels of graphic thinspiration, at par with the pro-eating disorder anorexics with the more profound level of disorder. Yet the motivation behind the level of graphic display is a vital place to differentiate between the groups. The pro-ana groups idealize emaciation as an image of will-power and strength whereas the pro-choice groups idealize emaciation because their members' consumption with self-loathing makes them wish to disappear.

Similar to other online communities, the eating disorder community makes use of certain features unique to the internet.

Community Features: Many sites use interactive tools such as message boards, chat rooms and even personal advertisements for "buddies". The topics on the message boards are organized around the above mentioned topics and include tips and tricks, nutrition information and thinspiration. However these boards also give members the opportunity to share their own stories, find sympathy for their daily struggles, and celebrate their success with those who share their goals. Some boards are specified for "resolutions" and here members can post their weight loss plans and progress.

It is common for members to join group plans. An especially popular group activity is fasting which generally requires the ingestion of only zero calorie beverages such as water or diet soda. Group fasts may be for a specified period of time or may continue indefinitely on the basis of competition between the fasters.

Message boards also provide a forum to share "stats" for the purpose of comparison between members. Stats include age, current weight, goal weight, lowest weight, highest weight, and height and body mass indicator. Several goal weights may be posted with indication of deadline for each respective goal. Many have clearly stated short term goals but are ambiguous of where their weight loss may be satisfactory. Final goal weights are often posted with a question mark.

Below is an example of how these stats are generally organized:

Age: 18

bmi: 20.64 (ew!)

h: 5′4′′

cw: 120lbs (disgusting!)

hw: 140lbs

lw: 118lbs

lgw: 100lbs (July 20)

2gw: 90lbs (August 20)

fgw: never?

Chat rooms are eagerly propagated by members who feel unable to share their feelings openly in offline forums. Chat rooms are usually linked to specific sites and require a sign-in name. Few chatters use their legal names, opting instead to reflect their personality through their online tag. The integration of disorder label is popular; rooms are filled with names possessing "ana" or "mia", for example "AnaPrincess". Chatters also name themselves according to their hopes, fears and indirectly related interests, for example "SkinnyDancer" or "FatWannaBe". Finally chatters label themselves according to their immediate dieting success or failure. Fasters may state the number of hours that they have been fasting ("←hr63!") and those who are failing at their diet plans use their sign-in name to confess their sin ("justatecake").

While many preserve their anonymity by choosing a new name each time they enter a chat room, others develop their online personality by keeping the same name throughout their interaction with the online community. By maintaining a permanent name members can forge friendships and even maintain online alliances. It is not uncommon for a chat room to be divided by support for and support against a prominent member or for prominent members to informally divide chat time to provide enough opportunity for each to lead the discussion without contradicting each other.

On the rare occasion that a male should propagate the site, they tend to indicate their gender within their sign-in name and often do use their legal names. Males in chat rooms take near celebrity status and are a source of constant interest and flirtation for the females. Regardless of disorder the young group expresses a desire for sexual attention, even if only under the distance and safety of anonymous chat rooms.

Despite the occasional personality conflict or power struggle, the message boards and chat rooms serve as a safe haven for surfers. Hostility is difficult to sustain in this environment because it is stifled by members who favor treating each other with the love and respect. In fact one of the most striking impressions gained in the analysis of the eating disorder community is the genuine state of sisterhood between propagators of sites; they love each other, cling to each other, like refugees from a broken state. Accordingly, negative reinforcement or even criticism is generally unacceptable on message boards and no chatter in need is ignored; while every comment may not gain a response, statements expressing emotional strife ("I'm so lonely!") are always met with concern and support.

The highest level of support is found in ana or mia buddies. Buddies can be found informally through message boards or chat rooms and formally through buddy personal ads. Personal ads list stats, disorder and goals. Ana or mia buddies usually share these three items in common.

On the other side of the spectrum of support are areas where members can post their original poetry and prose. The following is an example piece written by a member of the online community, submitted with the hope of enlightening those outside of the community to the private daily struggle many members face.

Yogurt on the Hour

By Jaci

120 calories and no fat. That couldn't be right. I read it again, checking the ingredients, trying to make sure that it wasn't a trick. It wasn't a trick. There were only 120 calories in the strawberry banana yogurt, none of which were from fat. It was almost too good to be true.

I opened the top slowly, letting the aroma swarm around me, the sweet smell catching me off guard. I dipped the edge of the spoon into the cup, piercing the gelatinous formation sitting inside. I dipped the spoon in deeper, then pulled it out after

I thought that it was coated with enough yogurt.

This was the plan. I would get 1 spoonful of yogurt, every hour, on the hour, and that would be my meal for the day. No more, no less. It was 8:00 am. If I went to bed at 10:00 I would get…14 spoonfuls of yogurt. Yeah. That sounded right.

I held the spoon up to my face, staring at the treat as it jiggled and moved on the spoon. I extended my tongue towards the pink goop and let a little touch the tip of my tongue. The sweetness was overwhelming. I let the taste linger on my tongue before I pulled it into my mouth and swallowed. Slowly I licked the yogurt off of the back of my spoon, savoring the sweetness and creamy texture.

After I had cleaned the spoon off, I replaced the yogurt in the fridge with a heavy sigh. If I jogged for 1 hour, by the time I came back it would be time for another spoonful. I stretched, extending my arms high above my head, then towards my toes. I performed my familiar stretching routine in time to a new beat: yo-gurt, yo-gurt, cream-y, cream-y.

I had only planned on running for one hour, but my legs kept me going to an additional hour. It was 10:00 am before I came back home. I showered quickly, watching my hair swirl down the drain, as usual.

I had forgotten all about the yogurt.

I dawned on me that I was overdue for two whole spoonfuls of yogurt. I stepped on the scale, trying to decide what to do. 92lbs. Still 2 pounds away from my goal.

Yogurt…

If I had gone this long without eating anything, if I had gone this long on one spoonful, what was keeping me from going another hour, and another hour, and another!

I went to the library. I didn't even go to the kitchen after my shower. The yogurt would have mocked me and tempted me from the back of the fridge. Instead, I sat in the library, researching my disease as if looking for a cure.

15% below the recommended weight… family dynamics… emaciated…yogurt…What? Not the yogurt again. If I had something to drink, maybe the cravings would go away. It was already 12:00. That's already 4 extra spoonfuls of yogurt. My mouth watered.

I went to the bathroom, searching for the water fountain. I took two sips, trying to concentrate on the coolness of the liquid. It wasn't working - the thoughts about yogurt remained.

I finally got home at 1:30.

5 spoonfuls. Greedily, I reached for the tub in the back of the fridge. I lifted the top up and stared at the jiggling treat. Slowly, I repeated the action that I had

performed earlier - tasting it first on my tongue, then licking the spoon clean. After the 3rd spoonful I grew fearful of losing control. It just tasted so good! I licked the spoon off and then replaced the yogurt in the fridge. I couldn't make it to the 4th and 5th spoonful. What if I couldn't stop after the 5th?

I ran to my room and locked myself in, turning my stereo up to full volume and dancing like a maniac.

My mom came home from work at about 6 and left me a bag full of fast food. She said something about how I never ate enough and made me promise to eat all of dinner. I said that I would as she exited the house, returning to work.

I lied. Sort of.

I chewed the food, letting it sit in my mouth for a minute or two before spitting it out into the toilet and flushing it away. I couldn't bring myself to swallow it.

All I really wanted was the yogurt. All I really needed was the yogurt.

I watched a few of my favorite anorexia movies, rewinding all of my favorite parts over and over. One of my teammates called and told me about some meeting after school on Tuesday. I didn't care. All I could think about was yogurt.

The hours passed with agonizing sluggishness.

9:00 came and went. I had gone all day on 4 spoonfuls of yogurt. I deserved to have the rest! I had spent the whole day keeping time with that yogurt. It was time to reward myself.

I took it to my room, so that I could sit alone and eat it. I held the spoon over the tub, but I couldn't dip it in. I had gone all day on less than 30 calories. How could I mess up now?

With a heavy heart, I watched my creamy reward swirl down the toilet, diluting then disappearing in the water.

It didn't matter. I didn't need it after all. I didn't need anything. 30 calories is pretty good. It's pretty darn good!

I was proud of myself. I was stronger than yogurt and fast food and genetics and biology and everything.

10:00… time for bed. Was I really proud of myself?

Sacred Texts

A Letter from Anna

Allow me to introduce myself. My name, or as I am called by so called "doctors", is Anorexia. Anorexia Nervosa is my full name, but you may call me Anna. Hopefully we can become great partners. In the coming time, I will invest a lot of time in you, and I expect the same from you.

In the past you have heard all of your teachers and parents talk about you. You are "so mature", "intelligent", "14 going on 45", and you possess "so much potential". Where has that gotten you, may I ask? Absolutely nowhere! You are not perfect, you do not try hard enough, further more you waste your time on thinking and talking with friends and drawing! Such acts of indulgence shall not be allowed in the future.

Your friends do not understand you. They are not truthful. In the past, when the insecurity has quietly gnawed away at your mind, and you asked them, "Do I look…fat?" and they answered "Oh no, of course not" you knew they were lying! Only I tell you the truth. Your parents, let's not even go there! You know that they love you, and care for you, but part of that is just that they are your parents and are obligated to do so. I shall tell you a secret now: deep down inside themselves, they are disappointed with you. Their daughter, the one with so much potential, has turned into a fat, lazy, and undeserving girl. **But I am about to change all that.**

I expect a lot from you. You are not allowed to eat much. It will start slowly: decreasing of fat intake, reading the nutrition labels, cutting out junk food, fried food, etc. For a while, the exercise will be simple: some running, perhaps some crunches and some sit-ups. Nothing too serious. Perhaps drop a few pounds, take a little off of that fat tub of a stomach. But it won't be long before I tell you that it isn't good enough.

I will expect you to drop your calorie intake and up your exercise. I will push you to the limit. You must take it because you cannot defy me! I am beginning to imbed myself into you. Pretty soon, I am with you always. I am there when you wake up in the morning and run to the scale. The numbers become both friend and enemy, and the frenzied thoughts pray for them to be lower than yesterday, last night, etc. You look into the mirror with dismay. You prod and poke at the fat that is there, and smile when you come across bone. I am there when you figure out the plan for the day: 400 calories, 2 hours exercise. I am the one figuring this out, because by now my thoughts and your thoughts are blurring together as one.

I follow you throughout the day. In school, when your mind wanders I give you something to think about. Recount your calories for the day. It's too much. I fill your mind with thoughts of food, weight, calories, and things that are safe to think about. Because now, I am already inside of you. I am in your head, your heart, and your soul. The hunger pains you pretend not to feel is me, inside of you.

Pretty soon I am telling you not only what to do with food, but what to do ALL of the time. Smile and nod. Present yourself well. Suck in that fat stomach, dammit! God, you are such a fat cow!!! When mealtimes come around I tell you what to do. I make a plate of lettuce seem like a feast fit for a king. Push the food around. Make it look like you've eaten something. No piece of anything… if you eat, all the control will be broken…do you WANT that?? To revert back to the fat COW you once were?? I force you to stare at magazine models. Those perfect skinned, white teethed, waifish models of perfection staring out at you from those glossy pages. I make you realize that you could never be them. You will always be fat and never will you be as beautiful as they are. When you look in the mirror, I will distort the image. I will show you obesity and hideousness. I will show you a sumo wrestler where in reality there is a starving child. But you must know this, because if you knew the truth, you might start to eat again and our relationship would come crashing down.

Sometimes you will rebel. Hopefully not often though. You will recognize the small rebellious fiber left in your body and will venture down to the dark kitchen. The cupboard door will open slowly open, creaking softly. Your eyes will move over the food cupboard door will slowly open, creaking softly. Your eyes will move over the food that I have kept at a safe distance from you. You will find your hands reaching out lethargically, like a nightmare, through the darkness to the box of crackers. You shove them in, mechanically, not really tasting but simply relishing in the fact that you are going against me. You reach for another box, then another, then another. Your stomach will become bloated and grotesque, but you will not stop yet. And all the time I am screaming at you to stop, you fat cow, you really have no self-control, you are going to get fat.

When it is over, you will cling to me again, ask me for advice because you really do not want to get fat. You broke a cardinal rule and ate, and now you want me back.

I'll force you into the bathroom, onto your knees, staring into the void of the toilet bowl. Your fingers will be inserted into your throat, and, not without a great deal of pain, your food binge will come up. Over and over this is to be repeated, until you spit up blood and water and you know it is all gone. When you stand up, you will feel dizzy.

Don't pass out. Stand up right now. You fat cow you deserve to be in pain!

Maybe the choice of getting rid of the guilt is different. Maybe I chose to make you take laxatives, where you sit on the toilet until the wee hours of the morning, feeling your insides cringe. Or perhaps I just make you hurt yourself, bang your head into the wall until you receive a throbbing headache. Cutting is also effective. I want you to see your blood, to see it fall down your arm, and in that split second you will realize you deserve whatever pain I give you. You are depressed, obsessed, in pain, hurting, reaching out but no one will listen! Who cares?! You are deserving; you brought this upon yourself.

Oh, is this harsh? Do you not want this to happen to you? Am I unfair? I do do things that will help you. I make it possible for you to stop thinking of emotions that cause you stress. Thoughts of anger, sadness, desperation, and loneliness can cease because I take them away and fill your head with the methodic calorie counting. I take away your struggle to fit in with kids your age, the struggle of trying to please everyone as well. Because now, I am your only friend, and I am the only one you need to please.

I have a weak spot. But we must not tell anyone. If you decide to fight back, to reach out to someone and tell them about how I make you live, all hell will break lose. No one must find out, no one can crack this shell that I have covered you with. I have created you, this thin, perfect, achieving child. You are mine and mine alone. Without me, you are nothing. So do not fight back. When others comment, ignore them. Take it into stride, forget about them, forget about everyone that tries to take me away. I am your greatest asset, and I intend to keep it that way.

Sincerely, Anna

Ana Creed

I believe in Control, the only force mighty enough to bring order to the chaos that is my world.

I believe that I am the most vile, worthless and useless person ever to have existed on this planet, and that I am totally unworthy of anyone's time and attention.

I believe that other people who tell me differently must be idiots. If they could see how I really am, then they would hate me almost as much as I do.

Eda R. Uca

I believe in oughts, musts and shoulds as unbreakable laws to determine my daily behavior.

I believe in perfection and strive to attain it.

I believe in salvation through trying just a bit harder than I did yesterday.

I believe in calorie counters as the inspired word of god, and memorize them accordingly.

I believe in bathroom scales as an indicator of my daily successes and failures

I believe in hell, because I sometimes think that I'm living in it.

I believe in a wholly black and white world, the losing of weight, recrimination for sins, the abnegation of the body and a life ever fasting.

Eda R. Uca

Ana Psalm

Strict is my diet. I must not want. It maketh me to lie down at night hungry. It leadeth me past the confectioners. It trieth my willpower. It leadeth me in the paths of alteration for my figure's sake. Yea, though I walk through the aisles of the pastry department, I will buy no sweet rolls for they are fattening. The cakes and the pies, they tempt me. Before me is a table set with green beans and lettuce. I filleth my stomach with liquids, My day's quota runneth over. Surely calorie and weight charts will follow me all the days of my life, And I will dwell in the fear of the scales forever

Introduction to Philosophical Factions

A common misconception about the underground eating disorder community at large is that all sites display the same message and most display the "pro-ana" ideal. In fact the underground community (as apposed to the "warning and recover" group which is far more easily accessed by the general public and better understood by the virtue of their mission) can ideologically be divided into two main categories: pro-eating disorder and pro-ana/mia.

Most members of the greater community formally, through identification, or informally, through displayed behavior and motivation, belong to pro-ed groups. Pro-ed groups encompass all eating disordered behavior however in the greater community people suffering through bulimia or identifying themselves as Mia are less represented than those who are anorexic or Ana. Those with other eating disorders, such as compulsive over eating are represented in even fewer numbers. There are several possible explanations for this.

The first sites were created by those who identified themselves as anorexic, drawing in similar members. Thus at its foundation, the greater community was created by and for anorexics. While bulimics are also food conscious and weight conscious, the act of vomiting is less easily romanticized than starving; take for example, the image of the "starving artist." Moreover, vomiting is considered to be a more specialized skill than starving and therefore not open to all community members. Indeed it is often thought of as the less preferred method of weight loss and is used as a compensatory rather than prolific weapon in the battle against fat.

Those who neither identify themselves with ana or mia behavior are further excluded because while they are both food and weight conscious, they share less with those who are starving or binging and purging. Their daily experiences remove them one more step from the anorexic core of the community. Since they identify less with the "hunger artists" of both ana and mia groups, they are less likely to use community features such as chat rooms or message boards.

While these categories are very useful in identifying major sites, webmasters, and other leaders within the community, they only serve as loose guidelines for understanding the ordinary community member. In fact there is a good deal of confusion among members as to how they themselves fit into these categories and although many identify themselves as part of one school of thought, very few are fundamentalists.

Pro-Eating Disorder Community:

My disease is none of your business!

The pro-ed community has members which identify themselves as eating disordered and admonish the suggestion that their daily struggle could be likened to a lifestyle choice. The choice that is being made by members of this community is to not formally seek recovery. While some teeter on a thin line between illness and health, many unapologetically indulge their disordered behavior. Likening their stance to those who are pro-choice in reference to abortion rights, members of this community view their eating disorders as a personal issue and abhor the irreverent intrusion of their families, friends, doctors, social workers, mental health workers and any other member of the offline community which tries to force them into recovery. They further claim that their online community has the right to express its world view and that shutting their sites down is a matter of censoring a minority that has no public advocate.

The pro-ed community can be divided into two subgroups defined by level of integration into the eating disorder community: the self-expression group and the communal group. The members of the self-expression group live in relative isolation while keeping web-journals. These people detail their diets, their goals, their failures and successes and may or may not commit their entire journals to eating disorder related material. These journals often include daily reflections, personal profiles, original art work and links to favorite pro-ed sites. By contrast, the communal group actively engages in all levels of community activities as outlined in the description of community features. The members of this group most value the emotional support that they gain from other members and the anonymity that meeting online provides. The following piece was written by Marna to help explain to the general public what she and others gain from inclusion to this group.

We Need a Place to Belong

By Marna

When I first heard about the existence of pro-eating disorder sites, I, like the rest of the general public, was horrified. At the time, I was the picture of recovery: I was going to therapy, taking my medication, and had been purge free for about 3 months. I was talking about my eating disorder with anyone who would listen, and finally expressing my feelings instead of throwing them up as I had been doing for the past 2 years.

I had heard rumors about these sites for a few months, but having not seen one myself, could not believe that there were actually people out there who would be calling an eating disorder a "choice" or a "lifestyle" and encouraging others to embrace it; it sounded like a twisted cult. I saw a story on them on my local news and while I was disgusted, I was also intrigued. Checking a site out could be a way of testing myself, similar to the way I would test myself around food throughout my disorder. *How much can I eat? How many times can I throw up? How long can I sit around food resisting it*? But this time the questions were more along the lines of; *can I look at these sites without falling back into the disease?* This was perhaps the most monumental question of all and I wanted an answer.

The next morning at work I typed "pro-ana" in a search engine. I was shocked by how many sites came up. Some glamorized the disease while others had clearly posted warnings that said the purpose of their sites was not to encourage people to "begin" an eating disorder but instead to offer support to those already suffering. I still couldn't understand it. It was yet another victory for my "recovered" self, as I looked at these pages shaking my head instead of thinking, "Yes, I understand that."

Fast forward to the next summer, approximately one year later. I had gained weight and that still terrified me, no matter how well I was recovering. I knew I couldn't turn back to purging because I had fought so hard to overcome it, but I needed to do SOMETHING. I thought back to the research I had done on pro-ana and pro-eating disorder sites and remembered the address of a few. I began to visit them, "lurking" on the messageboards. I tricked myself into believing that just watching didn't mean I was taking a step back in my recovery. For a while, that worked.

But I began to get desperate. I felt pressure to be the poster child of recovery. Everyone was so proud of my strength and let me know it by talking of nothing else. Valuing strength above all, I couldn't admit that I needed help. The well-intentioned praise forced me to retreat deeper into myself. I was full of pain and I wanted to talk to someone about it. I couldn't talk to my friends or family (god forbid they perceive me as a human instead of the super human I was trying to become) so I turned to the girls who could help me in my quest for perfection. I registered for a board.

Someone who is relapsing does not need disapproving looks, lectures or praise for how well they were doing. That just contributes to the guilt they are already feeling and makes them want to purge it from their systems. What we want is someone who understands how hard the fight is on a minute-to-minute basis. We need a place to belong. In these boards I found the support I was looking for. These sites create communities in which I don't feel like an isolated freak. The girls would let me vent about how much I hated my disease, how hard it was, but how necessary I felt it was. How I just could not see any other way in which to function. They never encouraged me to keep purging, but they recognized my feeling this way as valid, and they understood. They didn't look at me as many of my friends, family, and doctors did and ask, "Why don't you just stop if you hate it so much?"

The picture that the media has painted of pro-eating disorder sites is one where girls cheer each other on and try to prey on insecure girls who come to the sites looking for diet tips. This is not true. There have been many posts from young teenage girls saying "I want to try to be anorexic, can you help me please?? Give me all your tips!!" These posts are not met by the welcome wagon of the pro-eating disorder community. They are instead rapidly responded to, warning these girls that this is not something you "become", its not fun, its not a fad diet, it's a DISEASE. We are SICK and we acknowledge this. We do not want to lead anyone down the hellish path that we are taking. We encourage them to try healthy ways to lose weight and to stay away from our sites. If someone says she wants to stop and is ready for recovery, we are thrilled. We post messages of encouragement and wish them the best of luck. We all wish we had the strength that this person leaving the community does.

Something a lot of people don't understand about eating disorders is that no one will recover until they are ready to. You can take them to therapy and you can shove medication down their throat but it won't matter. I was mentally prepared for recovery for a while but I regressed. Without these sites and the support I receive from them, I feel that my relapse would be ten times worse than it has been. There are many days when I am overcome with "the urge to purge", and in these times I often sign on to a site and talk to the girls there. This both distracts me and calms me down as they reassure me that one binge will not make me gain ten pounds. I could not go into a normal chat room and start talking about this; I would be branded a freak, or, even worse, ignored. These sites help keep me sane and more in control, something of dire importance to a person with an eating disorder.

People think that by shutting them down they are doing something to help to cure the problem, but this is where they are mistaken. They are leaving those with eating disorders more alone, and this isolation is what causes so many of us to retreat even further into our obsession with food and calories. These sites by no means do anything to help treat the disorder, but they make it manageable, which is all those that are not ready for recovery are looking for.

Pro-Ana: It's a lifestyle, not a disease!

The pro-ana community does not claim that anorexia or bulimia is a lifestyle choice. They view those afflicted with eating disorders as victims of disease and contend that behavior rooted in disease is not a matter of personal control. Their connection with anorexia nervosa is that they wish to mimic the disordered behavior in order to reach their specified goals. The overriding principal of pro-ana behavior is the fulfillment of an individual's divine right to perfection through the maximization of personal potential.

Since the decision to take this path to perfection is a private one and each individual must create their own destiny, the pro-ana community does not attempt to recruit members. Indeed they feel that they are in the ranks of an elite community driven by a warrior ethic to success and that most people are not strong enough to be among them. Their manipulation of anorexic tendencies and glorification of thinness, control, austerity, persistence and endurance does not win them favor with the pro-eating disorder faction, which in contrast views themselves as diseased.

The pro-eating disorder faction feels that pro-anas are at best delusional anorexics that refuse to admit that they have a problem and at worst misguided and immature people with the time to create drama for themselves and the audacity to mock the struggle of true anorexics or bulemics. The pro-ana faction has to negotiate the paradox of pitying the eating disordered for their lack of control while still admiring the successful outcome of their uncontrolled behavior.

Thus, pro-anas do not validate eating disorders because each group identifies themselves as motivationally different from the other. The two camps live in uncomfortable peace, united by similar secret behavior, similar online and offline community members wishing to stop their behavior and a fierce sense of the right of an individual to freely express their beliefs.

The pro-ana community has a highly formalized set of goals and values. This may be because they are more sophisticated than the greater community and this may also be because their community exists more in writing than it does in action. Becoming or remaining thin is undeniably the primary focus of pro-anas. While other ideals come into play, the perceived sheer beauty of emaciation is a constant topic of discussion within the community. Beyond celebrating the aesthetic value of thinness, pro-anas claim that thinness is a reflection of excellence in other areas of one's life.

Thinness is the cellular manifestation of controlled behavior. Self-control is vital to the path to perfection because one cannot maximize her or his potential without fighting the urge to indulge in short-term pleasures. Since pro-anas are choosing a lifestyle which is difficult to sustain, they need constant external motivation and validation to successfully mimic the behavior that anorexics display unconsciously as a symptom of their disease.

Part of their lifestyles is reactionary to the consumerist culture that pro-anas find themselves in. Thus many have chosen to literally "eat to live, not live to eat" as a spiritual or political statement. These individuals are in a state of silent protest against a world which they perceive as overly indulgent or greedy. In fact, some are in less than silent protest; several articles can be found on any pro-ana site calling for individual revolution against the SAD (Standard American Diet).

Two of the least addressed pro-ana values are persistence and endurance. These elemental ideals tend to stir a "because I can" attitude in a pro-ana and condescension toward anyone who "can't" mimic anorexic behavior. Since weakness and victim hood are loathsome characteristics, persistently enduring hunger pains, fatigue and vitamin deficiency is highly honorable.

Others

Ana as Religion

An offshoot of the pro-ana faction is a group which considers there choice of lifestyle a religion. Control, austerity, persistence and endurance are the four unwritten pillars of Ana. Ana is a monotheistic religion and followers pray to Goddess Ana. The sacred texts of this religion include the Letter from Ana, The Ana Creed and the Ana Psalm. Individuals may also write a Letter to Ana and an Incarnation of Ana. These texts are not used only by those who practice Ana religiously; it is rare that a site falling under pro-ana or pro-eating disorder does not include at least some of them. The distinction is drawn between those who practice Ana religiously and others by the faith in Goddess Ana as a true deity. The texts are posted without any listed author as though having descended from the divine. Practice is the individual duty of each follower and thus there is no communal religious activity. There are no special days of celebration or observance.

Warning and Recovery

Warning and Recovery sites are not the focus of this work, however, since they are an integral part of the online community and referred to by members of the online community, it is appropriate to illustrate how their sites match and counter pro-eating disorder and pro-ana initiatives.

Disclaimer: Warning and recovery groups use disclaimers to state they their sites are not supportive of disordered behavior but rather of those individuals who struggle with their disordered behavior.

Tips and Tricks: Warning and recovery sites may also have Tips & Tricks sections.

These describe the dangers of following the above mentioned methodology, i.e. laxatives do not aid true weight loss and may leave the chronic user dangerously dehydrated.

Thinspiration: Warning and recovery groups inactively display thinspirational tools. In an attempt to deglamorize eating disorders these groups post pictures of those suffering through the disease to a point of death. Yet to those who embrace the highest levels of graphic thinspiration, people who die from self-imposed malnutrition are exalted as martyrs and saints. Warning and recovery groups continually grapple with this paradox. Some continue to inactively display thinspiration, rationalizing that those who praise commitment to death may be too sick to save. Others stop posting any information that may be taken as thinspiration, wishing not to create an opportunity for indulgence in disordered behavior. Many sites shut down completely, finding that few in the online eating disorder community use their sites as tools for health and recovery.

In Their Own Words

While sociological analysis is a vital aspect of understanding the underground eating disorder community online, there is no substitute for personal exposure to the thoughts of those who patronize these sites. The difference is tantamount to reading about blood in place of witnessing someone bleed. Thus selected communications of one very popular site between June 2003 and October 2003 are displayed below. The site was chosen not only for its popularity but also because it is a pro-ed site and so its members accurately depict the common behavior of the greater community.

Included in this section are surveys and posts. While these communications are accessible by the general public, names and any other defining characteristics have been changed or removed from the text to protect the anonymity of those who belonged to the community features of this site. However, in an effort to preserve the integrity of the statements, no other changes have been made. While reading through the grammatical and spelling errors may require some initial adjustment, they are important clues in guessing what type of people secretly communicate on these sites and moreover illustrate some of the differences between online and offline communication.

The surveys represent members from the United States, Canada, Australia and Israel. The surveys and posts are likely to have been answered by some of the same members but the fluid nature of online membership and participation makes it most likely that many members chose only to reply to some questions. The displayed communication is not meant to be observed as a scientific report of this community but rather as a "snap-shot" of a specific incident online. The reader should thus focus more on the questions being asked, as they are representative of a commonly held sentiment among much of the online community, instead of the answers given, which are profoundly touching but indicative only of one member's personal experiences.

Surveys

Author of survey states:

I filled this one out about myself… but please delete my reponses and fill in yours. I'm writing this out of curiousity.

Age: 20

Weight: 118 lbs :(

Height: 5'9"

Temporary goal weight: 110 lbs

Average calories/day: @900

Foods you eat most often: fruit smoothies, light tuna, salads, low-fat bread

Methods in addition to Ana: diet pills, expresso, drugs, Mia

Best thinspiration: public places & seeing thin, attractive girls

Worst trigger to eat: bordom

Difficulties w/Ana: I hit plateus… I can't get ANY lower than 115

Age: 38

Weight: 130lbs :(

Height: 5'2"

Temporary goal weight: 100 lbs

Average calories/day: @300?

Foods you eat most often: food? ewwww… i mostly fast, but occasionally (2-3 times a week at most) i will eat tuna, cucumber, or a subway sandwich

Methods in addition to Ana: diet pills

Best thinspiration: fat disgusting gross people

Worst trigger to eat: happiness

Difficulties w/Ana: pizza, ocassionally, i just cant help myself.

Age: 16

Weight: 148

Height: 5’8”

Temporary goal weight: 105

Average calories/day: 700-1000

Foods you eat most often: chocolate and salads

Methods in addition to Ana: diet pills, mia, excercise

Best thinspiration: other large people or usually internet sites

Worst trigger to eat: being bored

Difficulties w/Ana: chocolate.. ah i crave it like ciggs

Weight: 135 lbs :(

Height: 5’2.5”

Temporary goal weight: 110 lbs

Average calories/day: it's between 500 and 700

Foods you eat most often: Fruits like apples, oranges, pears, and popcorn

Methods in addition to Ana: diet pills, expresso,

Best thinspiration: public places & seeing thin, attractive girls and seeing very fat people…

Worst trigger to eat: food in the dorm

Difficulties w/Ana: when I'm sore i don't exercise like I normally do

Age: 23

Weight: haven't weighed myself in a while…too scared

Height: 5'5"

Temporary goal weight: 110

Average calories/day: don't know anymore… since I moved home with my parents

Foods you eat most often: smoothies, veg, fruit, ff jello, ff pretzels

Methods in addition to Ana: diet pills, occational mia

Best thinspiration: public places & seeing thin, attractive girls

Worst trigger to eat: bordom, stress, period, tired

Difficulties w/Ana: I hit plateus and live home with my parents

Age: 21

Weight: 109 lbs :(

Height: 5'4.5"

Temporary goal weight: 94 lbs

Average calories/day: @750

Foods you eat most often: salad, sugar

Methods in addition to Ana: caffine, nicotine

Best thinspiration: talking with my super thin girlfriend

Worst trigger to eat: bordom

Difficulties w/Ana: goddamn donuts and chocolate!!!!!!:(

Age: 19

Weight: 101 lbs

Height: 5′6″

Temporary goal weight: 93 lbs (If it's possible)

Average calories/day: 1,000 or less

Foods you eat most often: Fruit, Vegies, smoothies, coffee, meat, sushi and chocolate sometimes…

Methods in addition to Ana: exercise, exercise, exercise

Best thinspiration: Being in a bikini/ swimsuit/ tight clothes all day

Worst trigger to eat: My boy and my coach make me eat :(

Difficulties w/Ana: She gives me little energy to exercise- and when I don't I pack on the pounds.

Age: 16

Weight: 110

Height: 5'5"

Temporary goal weight: 90-95 – but i would looove to be 80*!!!

Average calories/day: 700-1000

Foods you eat most often: chocolate and salads

Methods in addition to Ana: diet pills, excercise

Best thinspiration: any really really thin girl

Worst trigger to eat: being bored

Difficulties w/Ana: junk food... ugh*

Age: 17

Weight: i think it's 160 now… but it haveno ides

Height: 5'7

Temporary goal weight: 100 lbs

Average calories/day: 400

Foods you eat most often: diet chokclot things… like fudge- but with 60 cal per one. lots of vegyes- espicely zokini- and some cheeze

Methods in addition to Ana: smokes. ton's of gum. exsrise

Best thinspiration: others girls- and i hate to admit it, but allso a very close male friend of mine… and ana books. i also whatch ftv all the time

Worst trigger to eat: my whight- or thinging about it.

Age: 14

Weight: 110 lbs;\

Height: 5″

Temporary goal weight: 110 then 100 for now.

Average calories/day: 1,000 calories, 500 fat calories soon to be reduced to 900 calories and 400 fat calories.

Foods you eat most often: fat free pringles. toast. push-pops. *stop cravings=good*

Methods in addition to Ana: drugs, alcohol… nuthing else i

guess?

Best thinspiration: school. public places. tv. models. **Worst trigger to eat**: boredom, anger and stress.

Difficulties w/Ana: binging. cant seem to stop eating food. im such a fat ass. : \

Age: 19

Weight: 130

Height: 5′8.5″

Temporary goal weight: 120, then 110

Average calories/day: 500ish

Foods you eat most often: raisin bran, apples

Methods in addition to Ana: mia, caffeine

Best thinspiration: my older sister (looks almost just like me, but 30 lbs thinner!)

Worst trigger to eat: bordom

Difficulties w/Ana: gaaaaaaah! I hate lithium! It slows me down sooo much!

Age: 15

Weight: 155 lbs

Height: 5'6"

Temporary goal weight: 120 lbs

Average calories/day: between 500 and 800

Foods you eat most often: fruits…yogurt…tuna… soup

Methods in addition to Ana: diet pills, exercise

Best thinspiration: seeing thin pretty girls

Worst trigger to eat: when i'm depressed

Difficulties w/Ana: when i'm depressed i don't exercise and i binge

Age: 16

Weight: 92 lbs :(

Height: 5′5″

Temporary goal weight: 62 lbs

Average calories/day: less than 100

Foods you eat most often: diet pop, tea, coffee

Methods in addition to Ana: diet pills(not currently) and excercise and (only when needed,ONLY) Mia

Best thinspiration: Mirrors, clothes, clothes shopping

Worst trigger to eat: I dunno

Difficulties w/Ana: I get forced to eat and then I gain

Age: 25

Weight: 143, please shoot me now

Height:5'7.5''

Temporary goal weight:110

Average calories/day: 300

Foods you eat most often: diet pop, rice, pickels, salad

Methods in addition to Ana: exercise, diet pills, mia sometimes

Best thinspiration: skinny girls, mirrors, my husband, who has smaller hips than i do(but not for long!!)

Worst trigger to eat: boredom, time of the month shit

Difficulties w/Ana: husband watching me all the time, hospitalization

Age: 21

Weight: 95

Height: 5'1.5"

Temporary goal weight: 85 lbs

Average calories/day: under 600

Foods you eat most often: fruit and veggies, diet yogurt, low fat, low sugar cereal like shredded wheat

Methods in addition to Ana: diet pills, caffeine, exercise, purging sometimes

Best thinspiration: being around people who know about my ED; i don't want to be a hypocrite!

Worst trigger to eat: bordom, drunkeness

Difficulties w/Ana: I live with my parents!!

Age: 20

Weight: 136 lbs

Height: 5'6.5"

Temporary goal weight: 125 lbs or less

Average calories/day: veries

Foods you eat most often: fruit smoothies, fruits, salads, veggies, v8 splash

Methods in addition to Ana: exersize,

Best thinspiration: fat people & seeing them eat,,thin, attractive girls, christina aguliara, before she died her hair and gained wieght

Worst trigger to eat: bordom, stress, periods

Difficulties w/Ana: i'm like addicted to bread, chocolate, and cheetoes…

Age:20

Weight:87-92 it fluctuates

Height:5'5

temporary goal weight:79 (I would just nut my pants if i was 70 anything)

average cal/day:200 damn that gatorade!

foods you eat most often:ff jello, and frozen ff jello (decisions decisions)

methods in addition to ana:mia, diet pills (various), ipecac syrup + running til i pass out heh heh

best thinspiration: my fat ass fucking stomache

worst trigger to eat: stupidity

difficulties with ana: being sad and lonely

Age: 15

Weight: to fat to even let people know

Height: 5'4

temporary goal weight: 116

average cal/day: 300 im a fat ass and a pig

foods you eat most often: diet coke, if ihave to eat, whatevers easy to purge

methods in addition to ana: mia, loads and loads of diet pills, laxs, writing fat ass, etc. all over my huge body, burning my tongue, wow i sure am f%cked up

best thinspiration: this waif girl at my school, shes perfect, so thin and she has AWESOME collar bones, my goal is to see all of my bones like her

worst trigger to eat: icecream, but hell atleast it comes up easy

difficulties with ana: isolating myself so bad, my friends know i have problems also trying to find places to hide the "purge"

Age: 16

Weight: 127lbs (I know disgusting)

Height: 5'6"

Temporary goal weight: 100 lbs

Average calories/day: 600 or less

Foods you eat most often: fruit smoothies, salads w/o dressing, green beans lite bread hard boiled egg whites

Methods in addition to Ana: diet pills

Best thinspiration: pictures of Paris Hilton, any fat person

Worst trigger to eat: around family

Difficulties w/Ana: umm well i am a fat cow and i'm having trouble dropping my weight as fast as i did before

Age: 20

Weight: 127 and dropping

Height: 5′5.5″

temporary goal weight: 120…115…110…105…

long term goal weight: 100

average cal/day: i like to keep it @ or around zero. i'll usually eat 300-600 cals and then burn off around 800. it's easier now that i'm back in college. summer sucked.

foods you eat most often: apples, fat free pudding (80 cals), GUM, and string cheese (60 cals).

methods in addition to ana: i can't stand the thought of throwing up in general, so no mia tendencies. just restriction and exercise—lots of exercise.

best thinspiration: knowing i used to be 103. also seeing my stomach flat with my hip bones jutting out when i lie on my back is very motivational.

worst trigger to eat: cookies.

difficulties with ana: since i'm living on my own, it's hard to not want to buy everything i see in the food store. i try not to shop when i'm hungry and taking diet pills helps a lot. i'm so happy i finally found ones w/ ephedra in them again!! yay publix!! i had tried non-ephera ones before but they didn't do anything for me. they also tasted 100x worse. this is the first time in 6 months i've used ephedra and i love it.

skinny or overweiht?

I was just wondering if…. you would rather be super skinny and in the hospital of 5lbs overweight and leading an ordinary life. which would you chose?

CHOICE	SCORE
super-skinny! Definitely	8
um… too hard a question	0
overweight! you can always lose 5lbs, and more!	5

Total number of votes: 13

You became ana or mia for what reason?

Just put why you decided you're 2 fat;

CHOICE	SCORE
To be perfect	26%
To disappear	7%
To prove you could do it	15%
You want everyone to envy you	13%

You just thought you were too fat	20%
All of the above	11%
None of the above	5%

Total number of respondents: 25

Motion: What Is "Ana" to You?

CHOICE	SCORE
A Deadly Disorder	2
A Not-so-deadly Disorder	1
A Lifestyle Choice	2
A Lifestyle, but NOT a Choice	10
My Best Friend	1
A Goddess	2

A Cool Club	0
A Diet	0

Total number of respondents: 18

Motion: What does ana mean 2 u

Details: what draws u 2 ana? when u here ana, what pops in ur head?

CHOICE	SCORE
control	18%
perfection	22%
loosing weight	22%
revenge/2 hurt someone who hurt u	6%

slow death	4%
attention	4%
like the feeling	16%
other	8%

"Other"	All of the above
	makes me feel good about me
	not so alone
	punishment

Total number of respondents: 17

What is your goal weight?

CHOICE	SCORE
110-115	47%
110-100	21%
100-90	26%
90-80	5%
80-70	0%

Who is the most thinspirational to you?

CHOICE	SCORE
Gisele	4
Kate Moss	12
Jennifer Aniston	4
Jodie Kidd	2
Calista Flockhart	6

Total number of respondents: 46

Hardest food to resist?

CHOICE	SCORE
chocolate	19%
chips	10%
ice cream	12%
pizza	17%
cheese	10%
popcorn	7%
spaghetti	9%
Other	12%

Total number of respondents: 16

Your favorite distraction!

CHOICE	SCORE
Exercise	18%
ana journal	12%
reading	11%
drinking water/ coffee/tea	17%
watching tv	13%
other	18%
"Other"	8%

Total number of
respondents: 12

cleaning

daydreaming

paint my nails

visiting ana
websites

What is your Current Weight?

CHOICE	SCORE
under 70	0
70-80	0
80-90	0
90-100	0
100-110	2
110-120	2
120-130	3
130-140	0
140-150	0
150-160	2

160+	2

Total number of respondents: 11

How Much do you Have to Lose?

CHOICE	SCORE
Under 10lbs	0
10-20lbs	3
20-30lbs	3
30-40lbs	0
40-50lbs	3
50-60lbs	1
60-70lbs	1
70-80lbs	0
80-90lbs	0
90-100lbs	0

100lbs+	1

Total number of respondents: 12

Ideal BMI

CHOICE	SCORE
21+	0
19-20	0
18-19	3
17-18	6
16-17	3
15-16	3
below 15	1

Total number of respondents: 16

Eda R. Uca

What and or Who made you decide that you wanted to lose weight?

1. i couldn't stand the way i looked. i was huge

2. i got really self concious abd could barely leave the house because of how ugly i am so i got pushed to start losing the uglyness.

3. i just couldnt stand looking at myself anymore, ppl at school would tease me and i was just sick of being "chubby"

4. I want to disapear right off the face of the earth!

5. Just want to be skinny and accepted. Less nudging saying "oh she is so fat" blah blah. Also looking good, nice clothes, and I'm into ballet, gymnastics and skating, so…..

6. My mother's death, and childhood abuse. Fasting makes me go numb, dieting makes me focus on something else.

7. My Parents always made little fat jokes, i'm currently "normal weight" (whatever that is) but i am alot bigger than my siblings, they are all naturally petit, and i am not.

8. My self. My health. My faith. The Lord gave me this amazing body to take care of it, not to abuse it by overeating and getting fat.

Eda R. Uca

When I see others packing on pounds I think…

1. damn, don' they even realize……?

2. God she is so fat!

3. i can't wait to get to my goal so that they can think I have control even though i don't.

4. I'm probably okay and normal and I feel better about myself actually.

5. i'm so glad I don't look like that. eww all that fat!

6. POOR PEOPLE! If they only knew what I do, they would see how simple it is to eat w/o killing yourself.

7. what fat slobs, how can they just let themselves get fat, do they know there fat?, i also u se ity as motivation so i don't become like them

8. Yuck! Good think Im not…

Eda R. Uca

What keeps you motivated?

1. Anything by fiona apple, and alanis moresette. They inspire me greatly.

2. goal weight, thinspirational photos, gymnasts, ballerinas, skaters, needing to look good

3. i like listening to mandy moore cuz it gets me thinking about how thin she is and how i wanna be her. i like pink too, i think it's because her songs are so angry. i guess it helps.

4. I like to listen to punk rock when I'm working out…great beats keep me motivated.

5. I like reading triggering books, and going on pro-ana sites is also very inspirational.

6. If I am getting bummed I either go to pro-ana sites or I look thru my ana scrapbook.That way I keep my eyes on the prize of having a perfect body

7. thinking about what i will wear when i get to my goal.

8. reading ed books and writing about why i HAVE to be thin.

9. Scale, pictures, my sisters, myself in the mirror, clothes sizes.

10. The best little girl in the world… best book ever

11. thinspirational photots, anamia friends

12. upbeat music, and hearing of other peoples success stories…

Posts

Subject: no matter what…

By Hillary

I have decided that I have to be thin..no matter what my boyfriend says or what my friends say…I cannot deal with being fat anymore…i will not be happy with myself until I am thin…Today is a new day & everything is changing…whatever it takes I'm going to be thin..I have to be…

just thought I'd share my moment of absolute power that I'm feeling & hoping that it's not just a moment but a lifestyle change…

Hillary

By Ali

---

good luck Hillary, ull do it,

loves

Ali

By Jean

All right! Go Hillary! Live for yourself, not them!

Jean

Subject: 911 emergancy

By April

---

if anyone..ANYONE…is online right NOW…can u please email back and tell me i need 911 help right now…plllllleeeease? anyone!!!!?

By Nikki

---

yeah i am on my aim is ———-

Subject: Making a new plan

By Grace

Hey,

Wel i need to find something i can stick to losing 11 lbs a month FOR 2 months so i can be at 118 by november 30th/ f anyone has any advice please i need it. I cant seem to fast though and i dont want to fast this weight off you know? i want to get a good solid 7 day meal plan and work out plan worked out for myself so i cant screw it up and binge help me guys i need the help badly…

By Lisa

---

wow thats what i need

i made a meal plan a long time ago

but i dont use it much

maybe itll work for u?

just a suggestion

and u should go to www.workoutplan.com and

get ur workout!

heres the meal plan i made up

500-600

recipes included at the end…

Snacks- (all around 50 cal,choose 1 a day)

#1- 1 cup strawberries (45 cal)

#2- 1 carton low fat yogurt (50 cals)

#3- 1 medium piece of fruit (50 cals)

#4- 2 tbsp raisins (50 cals)

#5- 2.5 cups air popped or 94% fat free popcorn (50 cals)

#6- A fruit roll up (50 cals)

Breakfast- (all around 100 cals, pick 1 a day)

#1- 3/4 cup cereal (make sure it says 100-110 cals per 1 cup… like kellogs all bran flakes, cheerios, special K, Special K red berries) + 1/4 cup skimmed milk = 100 cals

#2- Sweet Eggs (see recipes) + 1 medium Fruit = 100 cals

#3-Omlette- 1/2 cup egg beaters or 1 medium egg + 2 tbsp chopped spring onion + 1/2 cup mushrooms

74.5 cals if u use egg beaters

88.5 if u use a normal egg

and 1/2 glass of orange, pineapple, or grapefruit juice = 100 cals

#4- Apple + 1 serving Peanut Butter Dressing for fruit (see recipes) = 100 cals

#5- Low fat Yogurt + 1 cup strawberries (if u dont wanna have them as a snack) = 95 cals

Lunch- (can also have for dinner, which would put u @ about 450 cals total for the day)

#1- 1 baked potato + salad (1 cup greens, 9 slices cucumber, 1/4 cup shredded carrots, 1/4 cup mushrooms + 2 tbsp Fat free italian dressing or 1 tbsp balsamic vinegar) = 149 cals

#2- A cup of tomato soup or any other soup thats 100 cals per cup + salad (same as salad in #1) = 149 cals

#3- South of the Border Pizza (see Recipes) = 150 cals

#4- Tuna Pasta Bowl (see Recipes) = 137 cals

#5- Easy Microwave Honey Glazed carrots (see Recipes) = 150 cals

Dinner-

~* If ur with ur family, have 200 or 300 cals too keep em off ur back … if u have 200 cals, itll be a total of 500 cals for that day … if u have 300, itll be 600 *~

If u arent going to have dinner with family, have one of the choices from lunch or choose one of he following 250 cal dinner ideas….

#1- 1 serving Rice (40 g) + 3 oz lean chicken, fish or beef (size of a deck of cards) + 1 tbsp canned sweetcorn + 1/2 diced red pepper & fat free vinaigrette = 250 cals

#2- 1 serving pasta (40 g) + 1/2 tbsp pesto sauce = 250 cals

#3- 1 baked potato + 1/2 a 205g can of baked beans in tomato sauce = 250 cals

#4- 1 bread roll + a low fat beef burger or chicken burger (both should be grilled) + shredded lettuce + a sliced tomato + 1 tbsp tomato ketchup = 250 cals

Bonus!

if you've been good, have a 150 cal dinner (from lunch choices) and the following for dessert

Exotic fruit sundae -

mix together 25g chopped mango, 3 peeled and stoned lychees, and 25 g fresh pineapple. Add a pinch of mixed spice and mix well

Spoon into a dish with a scoop of vanilla ice cream (or frozen yogurt) and serve immediately

100 cals per sundae

Recipes -

Sweet Eggs -

2 egg whites

2 tbls sugar substitute

1 or 2 tsp cinnamon

1/8 cup sugar free maple syrup

mix egg whites until stiff peaks form, then add rest of ingredients.

put mixture into a bowl and heat in microwave for about 1.5 or 2 mins then serve

many ppl say this tastes just like mcdonals pancakes but without all the fat and excess cals.

= 50 cals

Easiest Peanut Dressing for Fruit in the whole world -

40 cals a serving

1 tsp smooth peanut butter

1 to 2 tbsp water

1. put PB in small bowl and add water slowly, stirring vigorously with a spoon throughout until a smooth kinda runny paste is formed
2. spoon over chopped apple

also- i like to add the water, put in microwave for 15 secs then mix (i like it warm)

South of the Border Pizza-

4 each fat free Pitas for crust

1 cup harvest crumbles to equal 1/2 pound hamburger

1 medium onion

1 each sweet yellow pepper

1 clove garlic clove

1 can fat free refried beans (16 oz)

1 cup salsa

1 can chopped green chilies (4 oz)

2 cups reduced fat mexican blend cheese (8 oz)

tomatoes and lettuce to taste

put harvest crumbles, onion, pepper and garlic in skillet and cook until veggies tender. Stri in refried beans, salsa, chilies and chili powder. Heat through. Spread over Pita. Sprinkle with Cheese. Bake until cheese melts.

Top with lettuce, and tomatoes.

makes 4 servings

150 cals per serving, 1 g total fat

Tuna Pasta Bowl (my fave!!!)-

makes 1 bowl-

Boil 60 g(2 1/4) oz penne pasta in lightly salted water for 8 mins.

Meanwhile, mix together 50 g (2 oz) drained, canned tuna, 25 g (1 oz)

sweet corn niblets and 1 tsp olive oil.

Drain the pasta and add to the tuna mixture.

Toss well and add 1 tbsp

chopped flat leaf parsley. Season

137 cals per bowl

Easy Microwave Honery Glazed Carrots-

Eda R. Uca

Ingredients -

.5 tsp cornstarch

1/8 cup orange juice

.5 tablespoon honey

.5 tablespoon butter or magerine

1/2 tsp grated orange rind (optional)

half a can of sliced carrots (7.5 oz)

Directions- combine cornstarch and orange juice. microwave on high for 30 secs- 1 min

stir to blend

add honey and butter and microwave for an additional 30 secs - 1 min or until sauce is thickened and clear. add orange rind

set aside

microwave carrots until hot, drain

pour sauce over hot drained carrots and mix well. reheat to desired serving temperature

150 cals

By Lindsey

---

hmmm..i prolly am lucky if i average 200 cals a day, and like maybe maybe maybe 20 fat calories a day? if that even? i'm down to 131 now, from 195, i lost so much wieght while my boyfriend was away for 8 weeks, that he says i feel funny now, he says i got no ass, my boobs shrank, my ribs stick out, and i have no shape, he hates it, but i dont care, he can bite me, i still have 25 lbs left to go to get down to 104, i've basically starved so long now, that ive averaged a 5 lb loss per week for the last three weeks, it rocks, course, i dont really feel to well lately either, and im growin hair on my butt and my tummy but i dont really care, cuz i will be the absolute thinnest that anyone has ever ever seen me, in another 7 lbs, i will wiegh less than i have since i was 12, and i'm 35 :) i only wear a 29 waist in levis, and i am so so so proud of myself, but you know, i really cant talk to anyone but you guys about it anymore, because my friends nd what not are gettin ready to like drag my stupid ass off to the hospital, so now im wearin baggy clothes, and trying to act like im eating, and you know, i think they all suck, cuz its my body, and i shouldnt have to have it fat juss to make them happy…grrrr….

By Sally

Watch your calories. Make yourself meal plans, and eat slowly. Thats what i do, thats what im trying. I used to eat 1000 calories, 500 fat calories, and now im trying to lower it to 800 calories, 400 fat calories.

By Lydia

---

keep you cals however low you can stand to make them and then be sure to

exercise all (or at least almost all) of what you ate. that way you're still eating but burning it off in the end.

By Laura

---

your so amazing Lindsey… i seriously wish i could have the modivation and determination you have! its great!! ::jealous::

I'll just be large large large forever!

By Erin

Lindsey-

I agree with the part of your e-mail where you talk about ur friends ready to drag you to a recovery center. I'm getting the exact same thing. I swear if I have one more person tell me I'm too skinny and ask me all these "concerned" questions, I'm going to choke someone! It's my damn body, and if I think I'm fat than back off and let me do what I need to do! I'm an adult and I refuse to let someone drag me off to the hospital where they will force me to eat and get FAT! My guy says the same thing - that i've lost my boobs. that's fine by me! the baggy clothes don't work on him cuz he can feel all my bones when he touches me. oh well!!

Ana Love,

Erin

Subject: my goal

By Marissa

---

hey guys. here i am sitting on my fat ass writing a post to u guize while im eating my 280 calorie soup. I made it cuz i thought i wouldnt like it but evidently anything tastes good to me. I'm not gonna eat the whole thing tho… no way in hell will i let myself eat the whole damn thing. I wanted to let u guize know about my new goal. My birthday is coming up… its october 8th. And I wanted to give myself a present that present is losing as much as i can… I'm thinking that that will be about 5 pounds.

But god I wish i could lose ten. I rele want to accomplish this but i have to do it by restricting not fasting… usually i have one meal a day. which is my after school snack which usually is a meal. Today it wuz 3 strips of calamari… not huge strips… maybe as big as ur average french fry and the soup im eating rite now.

I dont think i can restrict nemore for now i have to go down in steps… i cant go from 2 to 3 meals a day (ahh) to fasting. Hell I cant even fast. But im hopeing that if everyday i limit my calorie intake just a little bit more i will be able to fast… today im allowing 500 calories. i've had 220 cals so far and i plan not to eat nething else so maybe i wont get to my 500 cals.

Do u think i will be able to lose ne weight with my plan?

im so frusturated with myself :(

ana and mia hugs

Marissa

By Melanie

---

are you exercising too? if so, then its definately possible to lose the weight. when i stay under 400 or 500 calories and run every day i can lose weight fairly quickly. and make sure that the food you eat is also low fat.

good luck!

xxooMelanie

By Stephanie

Hey everyone. I normally don't post, but thought that today would be a good day to do so. Just to update evryone, I weighed in at a HUGE 172 lbs in May (birth control and depression did it) well I finally got down to 142 in august and kinda didn't lose anymore. Well I've been so disgusted with myself that I decided that I have to get out of this Horrible body. I don't eat anymore than 400 calories a day, but my roomate and my ex make me eat, so it had been hard to lose any weight with them around all the time. Thank God school started cause now I can claim that I ate at school or at work.

Well anyways, on wednesday i weighed 142.5 and this morning i weighed…….138.5!!!!!!!

YAY! Well I just thought I'd post some good news…basically you all inspire me everyday with all your posts, thankyou.

I weighed 128lbs in this pic

Height: 5'6

HW: 172

LW: 115

CW: 138.5

Goal Weight 1: 125

Goal Weight 2: 115

By Marissa

---

i ran a mile today :)

Beat all the girls in my class… i dunno if thats a big accomplishment but I wanted to beat all the girls i wuz rele determined so i did it :). altho i got an asthma attack after.

I excerscise everyday.

ana and mia hugs

Marissa

By Lindsey

---

keep up the good work Marissa :o)

i wanna weigh 104, im figurin at the rate in goin, it will definately be by christmas!!! yayness!!!

Lindsey

By Lydia

---

omg birth control can totally make you fat. i used to be on this one brand (sorry i forgot what it was called) and it made me gain 15 POUNDS. it completely destroyed my life. now i'm taking a different brand though called Yasmin which is really really good. it's a special kind of pill that specifically promotes weight loss. i love it. so if you're going to go on the pill, thats what i'd suggest. i lost all the weight the previous pill made me gain and then some :)

Lydia

By Lindsey

---

when i brushed my teeth last night, my gums started bleeding really bad, not just a little, but like all my gums, in my whole mouth, anyone else have this problem? and what do i do about it? i'm also late on my period, again, i was late by two weeks last month, and im about a week late so far this one. i take oodles of vitamins, what could i possibly be missing? and yes, i have been fasting, a lot

in the past three weeks, i think ive ate like maybe 4-5 times total?

Lindsey

By Laura

---

my gums bleed only when i brush my teeth after purging, but never regularly…. I've had messed up periods as well! gr, keep up on your fasting, your such a thinspiration!!!

-Laura-

By Marissa

---

ur gums bleeding may not be from ana.

My mom went thru that and she ended up having a gum disease. But who knos ana could have something to do with it… unfortunatly i don't kno a lot about it sorry.

Ana and Mia Hugs

~Marissa

By Angela

Hey Lindsey,

All this is normsl, soooo annoying, but normal! My gums have started sporadically bleeding on regular intervals throughout the day, it's horrible. Also, my periods arebeyond messed up! I'll not come on 4 3months & then be on for like, 2weeks &stuff!

Subject: periods

By Hailey

Okay this may seem silly but i just want to know if i am normal

Do you have a period?

If not, do you think thats a good thing?

If so, is it regular?

Eda R. Uca

How has ana affected your cycle?

sorry, but i havent had one for 7 months!

By Sally

If your sexually active, take a test, if it comes out negitive, talk to a doctor. If your not sexually activie, id say talk to a doctor. But then the whole ana/mia thing comes in and that makes you lose your period alot if you are deeply commited to it.

so theres a few questions you have to ask yourself.

my friend was sexually active and wasnt pregnant and just got her period, light though, after 5 or 6 months but shes nothing close to ana, so who knows, it could be normal?

good luck!

-Sally

By Julia

> Do you have a period? Yes, yes I do :(

> If not, do you think thats a good thing? -

> If so, is it regular? Yes except when Im heavily training sometimes it will be a bit lighter or come a little bit later

> How has ana affected your cycle? Its lighter- Im not sure how long I've been ana so i cant be certain- it feels like my whole life…

7 months is a long time- youre so lucky!!

By Mary

---

sorry to butt in on this one but my periods stopped for 10 yrs and I now have brittle bones and have bone density scans all the time!

It's not good but I'm still ana much to the disgust of my doctor. I told him ana was a life long commitment not just something you stop doing at the fist sign of trouble. I'm in this to die and make my parents, especially step father and ex-husband pay for my life!

Love

Mary

By Melanie

________________________ugh, i just started mine today and it's so heavy! gross… but usually i get them every other month. when i was at a lower weight they were more random and lighter. another reason to lose weight, i guess. i would love to just stop them altogether, even though i know its bad for my bones.

xxoo melanie

By Alicia

OMG I COULDNT HAVE SAID THAT ANY BETTER MYSELF MARY!

Subject: :(my boy/f hates me!

By Hailey

---

my boy is threatening to break up if i dont gain weight! we were fooling around in my room today and he had to leave because he was so repiulsed by my ugly body- he says i look like a little girl.

then says he used to love my body, but i now i look like i have cancer. im still fat though

weve been together for almost 3 years and i dont want to loose him- but i WONT get fat for him. i love ana too much. and i still have 6.5 pounds to loose!

:(why does everyone want me fat

By Julia

Wow that is so harsh… If he is your boyfriend he should love and respect you for who you are. That is just as bad as telling someone they need to loose weight.

My boyfriend loves ana and the way she makes me look. Im sorry, but this bloke has to go.

xoxoxo

By Lisa

____________________________how tall r u and how much do u weigh

By Melanie

---

i'm really sorry about your relationship. it sucks that your boyfriend doesn't accept your body the way it is, but at least you know he cares about you. maybe you could talk to him about it more and try to help him understand ana better.

xxooMelanie

By Ali

---

i don't think that he is right for you- if he is making a big deal about- your body.

love is not phiscal- it's spirtul.

Subject: my random thoughts

by Francis

It is time to take control and responsibility back from those who arguing about the right to answer.

We humans eat the diet of a lion, a giraffe, a pig, a horse and an ape. And not only do we eat the different diets of all these animals, but we do so at the same meal!

The sugar demon grabs you by the throat and you can't shake loose.

Only one thing matters for the rest of your life. Does what you are about to put in your mouth contain carbohydrates?

What becomes really important is maintaining your state of perfection and the freedom that accompanies it.

Cookies, cake, chocolate and other sweets - avoid them like Satan!

A person who had died and been given proper mourning might then be butchered in much the same way as a pig, or else buried and left until the flesh is decomposed. In either case, the corpse was ordinarily dismembered by kin, who first removed it's hands and feet, then cut open the arms and legs to strip out the muscles. The torso would be opened to remove the viscera, and finally the head was cut off and the skull fractured to extract the brain. Little was wasted.

The Torianders eat alone retiring to their own hearths with their portions turning their backs on one another and eating rapidly for fear of being observed.

In a sample of sixty cannibal societies, about thirty-five percent roasted meat regardless of whether it came from kin or from strangers. Out of twenty-six cannibal societies who ate only unpredictably roasted or boiled relatives and strangers alike; they also baked them, smoked them or ate them raw. Cheese is the hardest food to digest and it contaminates everything you eat it with.

Remeasure. Re-weigh. Try harder.

Eat sleek.

Experiment - strive for perfection. Obesity never made it easy to take care of a household and a bunch of screaming youngsters.

We are overeating as we slowly starve to death on american junk food.

We're innocent victims of carbohydrate-itis, the insidious, invisible, all pervasive plague of our century. What causes it? Mainly sugar.

We're prisoners. Prisoners! That's right. We're prisoners of our taste buds.

If you make a pig of yourself, you will become one.

The same way a plant will reach for the light source from wherever it is located in a room, so your body will forever strive for perfection.
Because there's all this putrefaction, fermentation, and resulting acid, what actually is in the stomach is a mass of spoiled, rotting, foul smelling food.

Our laws must be changed to provide a proper way of eating for everyone. Political actions can cut carbohydrates for you.

Subject: Chart on what vitamins to take if ana

By Nikki

Hi!

I found this chart, it was on a recovery site BUT it is just a chart of vitamins we anas should take to stay outta the hospital, none of them will make you gain, I checked, oh, AND stay away from peppermint, it is an appetite stimulant.

NUTRIENTS

SUPPLEMENT SUGGESTED DOSAGE COMMENTS

Essential

Multivitamins megadoses Must be taken in extremely and high doses because they minerals are passed through the containing gastrointestinal tract potassium 99 mg daily rapidly and are poorly and assimilated.

Very Important selenium 200 mcg daily

and zinc 50 mg daily

Acidophilus Follow directions on label. Needed to replace or. Take on an empty stomach the good bacteria megadophilus so that it passes quickly lost from use of to the small intestine laxatives and/or vomiting

Minerals Needed to replace lost including 50-100 mg daily (essential) minerals

zinc Do not exceed 100 mg zinc.

Protein As directed on label. Needed to repair all supplement tissues. (free form amino acids)

VitaminB complex 100 mg 3 times daily. Helps to prevent anemia with Replaces lost Bvitamins

B12 injections 1 cc 3 times weekly

plus liver injections 2cc 3 times weekly.

Vitamin C 5,000 mg daily Needed for the

impaired in divided doses immune system and

to

alleviate the stress that is on the adrenal

glands

Kelp 6 tablets daily. Needed for mineral

replacement

Proteolytic Take between meals and To aid

in digestion and enzymes with meals. in

rebuilding of tissue.

Vitamin A . 15,000 IU daily Needed for repair

of all tissues and to aid the immune system.

Vitamin D

600 IU daily.

Prevents bone loss.

Vitamin E

600 IU daily.

Increases oxygen uptake in

the body for healing.

Have a good day…

Nikki

By Diane

Hey Girls,

I haven't been posting that much so I thought I'd tell yall whats going on with me :) Well I love school because I never eat anymore and I've lost 10 lbs. already and we're only going onto the 2nd week of school! LOL I'm HAPPY. And there's this senior (one of my brothers friends) and she is such a fucking thinspiration. She's anorexic and everyones talking about how disgusting she looks (shes emaciated) but I think she looks perfect. She thinner than most models I've ever seen.Everyone goes on saying "she needs help she looks sssoooo sick you can see every single bone in her back" which yes you can literally see every bone in her back but that is ssssoooo amazing. I just read my emails and I can't remember who wrote it but they said "think thin but healthy" I just gotta say FUCK HEALTHY I wanna be emaciated Hell i want to be MICHELLE STEIN she is perfect and I cant fuckin wait until people are talking about how "disgusting" i look. I hope she takes it as a compliment b/c she is perfect no matter what those morons say bout her. She exercises 4 hrs. each day and eats 3 salads a day but her salads only have lettuce and nothing else. SO WHO WANTS TO FUCK HEALTHY AND BECOME EMACIATED WITH ME AND MICHELLE??

Diane

By Hillary

Diane.. me! At this point I do not give a rats ass about my health. I'm not healthy. I'm so fucking unhealthy physically as well as mentally so FUCK IT ALL! Emaciation.. here we all come!!

By Erin

Hey Rachel-

I agree 100% with you! I could care less about "healthy" right now. All I care about is being super thin! Emaciated sounds wonderful to me!

Let's go girl!

Ana luvs,

Erin

By Hillary

I think we should start a group for those who are in it for the long haul and are hardcore.. fuck healthy!! (can you tell I had a bad day today??)

By Nikki

I do…! Count me in!! God I wanna be soo fuckin skinny that I am invisible and no one notices me, yet they cant help but notice and stare cause I am soooo fuckin skinny. I will do it, come tomarrow, nothing will ever stop me.

By April

I know I sure the fuck do! hehe

By Ali

Count me in, im in it for the long haul, healthy isnt an option any more.

loves

Ali

By Nikki

I do…! Count me in!! God I wanna be soo fuckin skinny that I am invisible and no one notices me, yet they cant help but notice and stare cause I am soooo fuckin skinny. I will do it, come tomarrow, nothing will ever stop me.

By Tracy

You guys can count me in! I'm so sick of being this way!!

always,

Tracy

By Erin

Hi again Dianel,

Yep, I'm still in this with you! I'm so damn sick of my body being so fat! I make myself sick! I swear that food is the devil! I wish I could run away somewhere where there is no food or people to make me eat. But, anyway, like you said WE CAN FIGHT THE URGE TO EAT! Food, hunger, appetite… I swear all that comes from satan himself! Screw being healthy, I want to be as thin as I can be!!! Lets keep encouraging eachother!

Ana Luvs,

Erin

Subject: Slow Suicide

By Francis

————————————————hey guys, i was just wondering if i can find anyone whose on the same page as me. my ana is slow suicide. I'm doing it so it will kill me. i want to feel myself going if you know what i mean. anyway i was just wondering if there is anyone out there doing the same?

By Grace

I understand how you all feel about that… I feel like that at times.. But my Purpose for ana, is so that i can feel the dizziness of life and actally be what is perfection. .If i die while im trying or get there… then it happens… I live for this disorder that's what I am basiclly

By Diane

Same here, yall might think thats crzy but hell what do I have to live for?

By Erin

Ana, for me, is having complete control. I feel that I have had so little control over so many shitty things that have happened in my life, so Ana is my best friend. Even though I hate it sometimes, I know that it's the one thing I have complete control over and it feels so damn good! Girls, we are in control of how our bodies look. That's a GOOD thing! It's hard to put all this into words, but hopefully I've made some sense!

Ana Luvs,

Erin

by Ali

---

hammm....

for me ana is my life.

my life- not my death.

i hate to hear that you feel like that.... :-(

By Hillary

——————————I like the mystery of it.. people are in shock and appalled when they hear someone is PURPOSELY starving themselves. Most people can't even go on a diet let alone completely cut out all food. People do NOT understand, how could you do it? And why?? They don't understand b/c they could NEVER starve themselves.. why would want WANT to not eat??? Because I am strong. I am stronger than most people. I've been through so much and I've got a steel backbone. I can take anything. I don't even get sick, and you'd think being undernourished I'd get sick easily. It's control as well as knowing just how far I can push my body… And I must say, as sick as it is, even tho I'm saying no no I eat, I swear I eat, the looks of bewilderment on the faces of those who just do not believe me empower me to continue on…

By Sally

________________________To Me, Whatever Youd Call The Way I Eat, Is a Fom of Perfection. I Want To Be Perfect. Its also control. everything seems to be so spontanious and random. I hate it. I like order and control. But i never get that. This is
my one way of anything even close to an attempt at perfection or control.
-Sally

Subject: off topic; really upset

By Hillary

---

hey guys. I've been really upset lately. It's really scary bc I honestly and truly don't want to live. I don't want to die, but I just feel so alone and hopeless that what's the point of living if I am to be so miserable? My mother hates me. Plain and simple. She cannot speak to me without screaming at me. She's so mean to me and it hurts so badly bc I don't understand. My sister don't care much for me either. We were playing a game today and I looked at the score pad and for me my sister wrote "Stupid" instead of my name and I almost had to leave bc I almost started to cry. I mean what kind of crap is that? For no reason she wrote that. Everyone else's name was written, but mine.

I don't have much to do with my dad, but every time I get upset I think of him and even tho he doesn't want me, I still want to try. I think of calling him or writing, or emailing. I emailed once and poured my heart out and he ignored it. So today I was just so upset and so close to losing it that I thought what the hell and called him. He told me it was all my fault! I was only bearly 4 when he left, how is it my fault? He got another call so when he switched to answer it I hung up bc I was crying. I cut again, dammit. I scatched the fuck out of my arm. It burns so bad, and my whole arm is full of red blood marks under the skin. Hurts like a bitch, not that I'm complaining. It's nice to feel something other than sadness for a change. Well my father called me back when I'd thought he was just glad I'd hung up so he didn't have to deal with me. He really made it sound like he didn't want to be bother by me when I was talking to him earlier. So he said "You hung up" and I said "I didn't think you wanted to talk" and I'd been really crying so I know he could hear it in my voice and he almost yelled "I had to answer the other call!" and I was just monotoned and said "You were yelling at me telling me it was all my fault" and he said "I wasn't yelling at you, but I do have a few errands to run so I will call you back later." He did call from his cell phone so maybe he did.. but what errands does one do at 6:30 on a Sunday night? But whatever. If he calls, he calls. If not.. I'll still sit by the phone waiting. I wish I could let go but I still cry over him many nights and I'm almost 20. What the fuck is wrong with me. I wrote a poem to God last night. Here it is, after this I'll end the email.. thanks if you made it this far.

Dear Lord

Life to me has no meaning at all

It's a dark, cold place I've come to appall.

It's a chore just to make it through the day

Take me home, Lord, please take me home, I pray.

The don't need me here on Earth, I just sit and waste away

So it's okay if you come and get me today.

If you're worried how they'd react to my short-lived stay

The didn't want me to begin with so it will be okay.

I'm ready to go. I'm not afraid. I'm really sad, but I'm ready.

I'm ready to go away.

By Ali

---

hey Hillary….

i was reading you'r post just now… i don't know what to say.

i don't know you entire life story.

life-s a bitch. i know…. what can we do?

learn to evoid some people is a good idea to start. i hate my family. and it's mutoall- they hate me too. there ok form far away- but they kill me from the inside.

so i look for my love ells where. i write.

i thorw mysellf into music alot, i visit my friends (which are one of the most important things in my life), and hope fully will go into the army in the flowing year.

there must be one thing that makes you want to live for the next day- is'nt there?

about cuting.

i have'nt done that in months. but when i read your words....

i know what you feel. cuting is'nt pain full. it's kinda like ana. you can resiset the phiscal pain- and that makes you proud.

but... and this is a main reason for me- it's not pure. and for me that's what ana is. pure.

By Susan

Hey gurl,

cheer up. My parents don't like me eigther

i left my mom 7 months ago because she cared

more for a man that said that he would never marry here than she did for her on children, told me i was doing it for attention and blames my aunt who has been more of a mother to me that my mom for the most of my life. My dad up and left one day wasn't even planning on tell me and my brother… he moved four states away to wyoming, b/c the air is cleaner…that was his excuse.

i'm sorry this wasn't about my life it was about yours though. well i can tell you for a fact that if your parents didn't want you i can tell you that god did want you on this earth for some reason, or he wouldn't have put you here. and everyone in here wants you to live! We all love you. It dosen't matter what your parents think don't worry about there stupid irresponsible shit anymore. This is your life don't let them ruin it for you. Your worth so much more that that.

Subject: we''re not the only screwed up ones

by Hillary

---

okay now I will admit straight up that my mind is fucked up beyond repair. In all seriousness, I am killing myself. It's intentional as well as unintentional but either way I am starving myself. Whatever. I have issues, my mind is screwed up. It's got to be to be the way I am, to starve myself and I understand that. My mother. Lord help her for all the crap she's put me through. She always makes stupid little comments. Always has to throw in her 2¢ even when it isn't worth shit. Well, today she finally did it. "Look at your hip" she said. I bruise so easily, I've got the huge disgusting bruise on my upper thigh everyone points it out so I didn't even have to look I said "That's not my hip it's my thigh" and she said "Yeah, and a thunder-thigh it is" I don't think anything has hurt me more than that. Everyone else but my family has noticed my weightloss, 2 sizes in a month's time. I was thinking last night that I was ashamed bc I'm starving myself blah blah but now screw it. I am not even going to worry what anyone else thinks. How could she say something like that? Knowing all of this? I know she knows whether she wants to admit it or not. She's cold-hearted but she's not blind. I've never lost so much weight so quickly as this time and I haven't been this small in for ever and to say some shit like that? I just stared at her for like a whole minute, dead silence, then got up and left the room, didn't even finish the story I'd been telling. She says "Don't be such a baby, maybe you need some Zoloft" and turns on me so it's all my fault! Fuck her. I am more than ready to die so if she's not going to give me a reason to live than screw this shit, life is too hard anyways. I just won't eat period. Sometimes even though you know you can't

be helped, you still want their sympathy, someone to lean on to tell you you are worth it, they don't want you to die, etc.. In my life all I have is people more or less screaming hey, go for it! Why don't they care? I hurt so much inside and no one once has noticed and said "Hey, Hillary, what's wrong?" NEVER. It's so fucked up. I care so much about everyone else because I know what it's like to have people not ask "how was your day?" or "what's wrong?" or even "are you okay?" and not just refering to your headache because they're worried it'd affect how well you do your job. My bestfriend and I were in a fight over the same stupid guy for probably the 3-4th time, were not talking at all, she looked upset at work so I called her that night. I put forth the effort because I care, even though we were not speaking. Think she'd be touched or greatful that I noticed and was concerned? Nope. "Yeah I'm okay bye." Well fuck you, too, then. I have really really complained here in a long time. I'm sorry guys it's just so frustrating I am so sick of being alone. I'm so sick of this stupid disease. I swear if I read another "I just started being ana two days ago, can you help me…" email than I'm going scream. I don't know what's going on inside my head. I got up in the middle of the night last night to workout. I felt so disgusting because I ate ham and cheese on a hamburger roll that all I could do was sit there and cry because I just knew I was going to gain 10lbs if I didn't get up and make up for my greety self eating so much. I'm such a pig. Okay I'm really done ranting this time. If you got this far you are an angel, thank you for listening, I feel better. Ahhh.

By Erin

Gosh, I'm so glad there is someone else out there that feels like me. It's been the same all my life and you know what my Dad has the nerve to tell me?

1. It's just an attitude problem, you don't need medication!

2. Just diet and exercise, it will go away!

That is not what I need right now! They say that I just want attention. But, the fact is that I've had attention all my life, but it's the sickening kind. The kind that makes you want to die rather than hear them say it one more time. Why don't you work out more? You have issues? What are you manic depressant? I hurt and scream and cry, and in the end it's all my fault. This is pointless.

Yeah, I know just how you feel.

By Laura

---

hey hun.. I'm not going to say i can relate to you, cuz i can't imagine what it feels

like to hear that from your own mother. I do know what it feels like to go day-to-day without a simple, 'how was your day' so.. I'll just offer my support to you..you can IM me ANYTIME! Hope things get better!
-Laura-

By Lydia

Hey! i just wanted 2 say i feel the same way. i get way 2 much attention, especialy since my parents found out that i have "issues" im bipolar and have been in the hospital for it 14 times. whenever a family member calls it always me they ask about first. god am i screwed up. tommorow i think im going 2 pierce my ear, just for the pain. i love pain. i live 2 punish my body, i guess that's why i love ana so much. why i just said all that im not sure so ill finish by saying, please don't do anything that u will regret. i have tried to kill myself soooooo many times i can't even keep track, but from all the hard times comes good time. if its not your time 2 go u won't, trust me, im an expert, u will just have regrets. if u want to talk ———— is the way 2 reach me.

good luck and try not to make regrets!!!

love ya!

Lydia

By Lydia

---

hey, my brain is totally fucked up 2. long story short, 14 times in psych ward, suicide attempt too many 2 count. we are all human and so we are born into human nature. the problem w/ that is that we tend 2 only care about ourselvs. some more than others. as far as i know we can't read minds yet. nobody can no exactly what u feel but we should be able 2 pick up on basic emotions. apparently the people who hurt us have either not mastered that skill yet or they are dead inside, my guess is #2 but hey. do what u can 2 stay around people who are not dead, but 4 the unavoidable just remember that when u r dead u can't know true happiness. because u can hurt, u can also feel true love, happiness, and joy.

just remember we are all here 4 u. if u ever need a shoulder, ———-

hugs cause u r loved

- Lydia

By Lydia

---

thats rele wierd, it never even crossed my mind that there r bipolar groups out there. im rele slow i guess. ill definatly try 2 find some now tho. right now im on seriquil, welbutrin, effexor, and lithium. i havent gained anything from these. probably cause welbutrin and effexor are anti depressants and they can make u loose a little weight if anything. ill tell u 1 thing tho, stay away from depakote, i was on it a while back and i gained like 20 lbs at least. thank god it made me sick so i had 2 dump it. my moms on it now and i always tell her how much weight he gained and how she looks pregnant. its not nice of me but oh well, i don't like her, thats another story. if u find any good groups, let me know

ana (and psycho bipolar) *hugs*

- Lydia

By Jean

---

ha. "pregnant" mommies. mine used to look that way, then she found out she's diabetic, and she lost about 60 lbs when she shaped up his diet to match.

i'm working on dropping paxil right now (it makes me batty, but if you quit it too fast, you see shit), and i'm on lithium. i used to be on zyprexa, but that's some nasty shit. i put on a good 20 lbs and felt like a zombie. -_- no fun at all. lithium hasn't really made me gain much weight, just seems to keep me from losing much. and it makes me reeeeeeeally thirsty.

i'll keep you posted on any groupfinding success i encounter (i'm such a bum for groups… it's silly!)

psycho + ana hugs

Jean

By Alicia

I'm sorry about how fucked up everyone has been to you I wish I could apologize for everyone else. I just want you to know that I'll be here and please! please! If you need to talk about anything you could talk to me! I would

be more than happy to be here for you. OH AND ABOUT THOSE "ANA'S" WHO ARE ALL "CAN YOU TEACH ME HOW TO BE ANA?" YES THEY ARE ANNOYING! i WOULD LIKE TO APOLOGIZE FOR THEM TOO. THEY ARE A DISGRACE TO ANOREXIA. Take care of your self and never give up b/c i won't. and lastly, smile :) for me? please?

Alicia

by Alicia

Im glad to hear im not alone as well. We'll show them! Any time I cried my family would say i just wanted attention. All my family does is plot against me behind my back not to mention all the gossip I've dealt with. Can you believe that through all my struggles all they ever did was say it was "a nother way to get attention"? What the fuck does attention have to do with my boyfriend breaking up with me or starving myself or (when i used to cut myself) cutting myself? I just hope noone else thinks i starve or cry for attention.

But it wont matter hopefully really soon i'll be dead. Thank you girls for being here for me.

Alicia

By Alicia

---

omg lydia i was hospitalized too! My parents never let me forget >:(only 4 times tho and it sucked!

By Lydia

---

what were u in 4? i was in 4 suicide 5 times, paranoia 2, and thinking i could fly (manic) 4, cutting 2, and some other messed up stuff 1. Not fun! thats ok tho cause it helped a lot!

- Lydia

By Nancy

Ummmmmmmmm, what did u mean by soon ull b dead? i dont want to get all up in ur buisness but that kind of worries me. i rele know what ur going thru, my parents think im all about attention to. ive had something like a breakup (not exactly, it was forced by my parents) put me in the psych ward. i used to b a cutter but im trying to stop. so far ive only relapsed 2wice. (ya, go me!) please email me, i just want 2 make sure ur ok.

_________-

- Nancy

ps i know u don't do this shit 4 attention, its a lot deeper than that!!!!!!!!!

By Alicia

Im not going to stop (with ana) until i die.

By Alicia

But ill live with it as long as possible.

Reluctantly.

By Melanie

---

i know exactly what you mean. i know that some people really believe that they only want to get to a certain weight and then they will be satisfied; and i think that's great. i used to think that too. but i know now that i won't be satisfied until i look like i'm dead. i had thought that 60 lbs would be enough, but even that is seeming kind of high now (i'm not even close yet, though).

i wnat to look like a skeleton. i want to be hospitalised. i want to literally starve to death. i've got problems.

xxooMelanie

By Marissa

I know exactly wut u mean Hillary. Sometimes I feel the same way. And I think the only reaason y thats not my goal is because im happy with my life and dont want to die. But if I got very depressed i would hope for the same exact thing. Not saying that u arent happy but thats just how i feel about it.

ana and mia hugs

Marissa

By Melanie

---

well, sometimes i'm happy with my life and other times i'm not..... i'm not sad and depressed all the time; usually i'm just numb. but i know that i'm slowly killing myself and i'm okay with that. i would never jump off a building or slit my wrists or anything, but i am unhappy enough to not care about my body and health.... i don't know if i'm explaining myself very well.... i guess what i'm saying is that i'm not happy with my life, but not in despair either. i'm just numb.

xxooMelanie

By Marissa

---

yeah I understand u Melanie.

Eda R. Uca

If I wasnt such a chicken and so afraid of pain im sure I would be hurting myself all the time.. like cutting or something else. My outlet used to be pills sometimes 17 advil a day. But I had a scary overdose ish problem with tylonel pm so i dont take any pills anymore. It rele made me realize that life is precious and im no where near ready to die YET.

But it also made me realize that when things arent going good and im not as happy as i am rite now i could go back to my pill problem or start doing something more serious like drugs. I'm sure all u girls have already been thru all this but since there is a big age difference im at a different time in my life then a lot of u. Sorry to go on about something stupid….

But i rele feel like i know where ur coming from about being numb. I feel so bad for my boyfriend because all the time im perky and happy and then all of a sudden i get in a down mood and i wont even look at him. Like today for example he wanted to know wuts wrong and i couldnt exactly tell him "Oh im just close to tears because i've been eating to much lately and pretty soon im gonna be a fat cow and u wont want me nemore." i had to hide it and sometimes i hate that i cant get things out.

But thats wut u girls r here for rite?

well thank you for reading… sorry about this whole thing. kinda stupid yes i know.

ana and mia hugs

Marissa

Subject: somebody needs to kick me in the ass!

By Erin

——————————————AHHHHHHHH why is this happening to meeeeeeeeeee????!!!!! I have to actually eat lunch every day now because as seniors, we can have off campus lunch. So for the first couple days I was like no no no I'm not hungry, and then all of the sudden my guy friends are like "I'm buying you lunch, you never eat." But the thing is, I honestly don't look like I don't eat!!!!! I eat ALL THE TIME! When I eat, I get even more hungry. I guess it's now because I am exercising a lot more with cheerleading so my metabolism is up and I'm burning the calories, but still. So I need to be kicked in the ass SO bad. I'm going to get like a lot of Green Tea and I want to get diet pills but I don't know which ones to get.

AH sorry I am just SO mad at myself!

<3 Erin

By Melanie

---

kicks erin in the ass

come on Erin, don't be lazy! you can think of excuses to get out of eating, you've been doing this for how long? just because some guys are trying to make you fat doesn't mean you have to eat! JUST SAY NO!

kicks erin again

try to find something else to do at lunch. maybe go shopping or go home to "eat" or go to the library or the gym or something. then you don't have to be around people who make you eat. during my breaks at school i go running

or catch up on homework or sleep. i avoid the cafeterias at all costs! Same thing at work; i try to come up with some errand that is urgent that i have to get done so i don't have to go for lunch.

kicks erin once more for good measure

hey, you asked didn't you? lol, i'm just trying to help out! :D
xxooMelanie

oh and about those diet pills, i prefer Hydroxycut cause they give me tons of energy. Xenedrine EFX supressed my appetite well.

By Ali

---

poor erin!!!!!!! i no the feeling.. i only eat wen i go to my friends house :'(

good luck, i still need ur sn

loves

Ali

By Angela

<applauds Melanie on that email!> Especially the 1st paragraph, we need more emails like that in here! Instead of just being all like "Oh it'll be ok, ull lose that weight soon :o)" etc…we've got into a pattern of that now & it's bad, we need 2 start telling each other the truth, it's not ok & we have 2 give each other thinspiration 2 lose!

By Melanie

---

lol, after i sent it i read it again and i was worried that i sounded like a bitch, but i was just trying to help out. i know that sometimes i just need a little push to help me along. i hope that you didn't take it personally, erin! but i'll do it again for anyone who needs a kick and i hope someone will do it for me too!

xxooMelanie

By Erin

---

awwwwwwwwwww i love you sooooooo much!

sorry it's been so long since I posted so you probably don't even remember what I'm replying to, but apparently I've been kicked in the ass 3 times, and I TOTALLY feel it!

I've put myself on some STRICT restricting rules until homecoming (september 15th). And whats really cool, is that I'm making my dress! It will be so pretty because I can never find anything I REALLY like in the stores and they always look so funny on me cuz i have a long torso and short legs so I was like whatever I'll do it myself, and it's coming along great. And I'm making it with a waist that 4 inches smaller than mine and hips that are 3 inches smaller than mine (my ass won't budge, and I can always take it in!!!!) Alright, sorry for gushing, but I will be posting a lot tonight! I'm going to catch up!

<3 Erin

Notes

About the Author

Eda R. Uca has been immersed in the online eating disorder underground for over two years. She is thrilled to be sharing her investigative work with the public and hopes that it will help break through the isolating misinformation which enshrouds the members of the online eating disorder community. In the future she looks forward to illuminating the position of other underrepresented groups as a means of bringing their cause to the forefront of mainstream society. She lives in Long Island, New York with her family.

Printed in the United States
51662LVS00005B/137

9 781418 437954